Your Local Area
SHOPS

Ruth Thomson

Photography by Neil Thomson

WAYLAND

First published in 2010 by Wayland

Copyright © Wayland 2010

Wayland
338 Euston Road
London NW1 3BH

Wayland Australia
Hachette Children's Books
Level 17/207 Kent Street
Sydney NSW 2000

Editor: Nicola Edwards
Designer: Edward Kinsey
Design Manager: Paul Cherrill

British Library Cataloguing in Publication Data

Thomson, Ruth, 1949-
 Your local area.
 Shops. -- (Your local area)
 1. Stores, Retail--Juvenile literature.
 I. Title II. Series
 381.1-dc22

ISBN: 978 0 7502 6085 5

Printed in China

Wayland is a division of Hachette Children's Books,
a Hachette UK Company.
www.hachette.co.uk

Free downloadable material is available to complement
the activities in the Your Local Area series, including
worksheets, templates for charts and photographic
identification charts. For more information go to:
www.waylandbooks.co.uk/yourlocalarea
<http://www.waylandbooks.co.uk/yourlocalarea>

Contents

What is a shop?

Shops sell food, clothes and other goods that people need or want. Some shops offer a service, such as watch mending, haircutting or dry cleaning.

There are many features that make shops different from other buildings.

? What service does this shop offer?

the name of the shopkeeper or what the shop sells

an awning to protect goods from the sun

an open door, so people can walk straight in

colourful paintwork

large glass windows, so people can see the display on show inside

Many shops also have signs hanging above the pavement, so people can find the shops easily from a distance.

? Can you guess from these three signs what each shop sells?

A local look

★ Take photographs of shops and shop signs in your area.
★ Decide which shops sell things and which provide a service.
Divide your photos into two groups like this and make a wall display.

Shops that sell things	Shops that provide a service

Shops that sell things

butcher

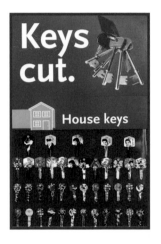

baker

hardware shop

gift and card shop

household and electrical goods shop

shoe shop

Shops that provide a service

Keys cut. House keys

AVAILABLE HERE
DRY CLEANING
★ ★ ★
LAUNDRY
★ ★ ★
IRONING
MONDAY - WEDNESDAY - FRIDAY
COLLECTION & DELIVERY

ISTANBUL IMAGE
BERBER SALONU
METIN ERDEM

'20 MIN' PHOTOS

★ What services do these shops provide? What others can you think of?

5

Come and buy!

Shopkeepers want you to come in and buy. They arrange colourful window displays or put goods outside to catch your eye and make you stop.

How do these two shops attract shoppers?

BETTER THAN
HALF PRICE SALE!

EXTRA 10% OFF FURNITURE SALE PRICES TODAY!

CARGO

WESTERN FRONT BOOKS

BOOK SHOP
OPEN

WESTERN FRONT BOOKS
96 HIGH STREET
WARE, HERTFORDSHIRE
PHONE: 01920 466 668

A local look

★ Notice what sort of shops have pavement displays.
★ Why do butchers and jewellers never display their goods outside?

food shop

4.99   9.99   7.99

shoe shop

Some shops, especially clothes and shoe shops, change their stock every week. They want to encourage shoppers to come back over and over again. Shops often encourage people to buy by offering goods at reduced prices.

? How do these offers and displays tempt shoppers?

DIY shop

florist

Your nearest shop

If you live in a town, your nearest shop may be a small store on the corner of two streets of houses. It will probably be run by a family. If you live in the country, you may have a nearby village shop, which is a post office as well.

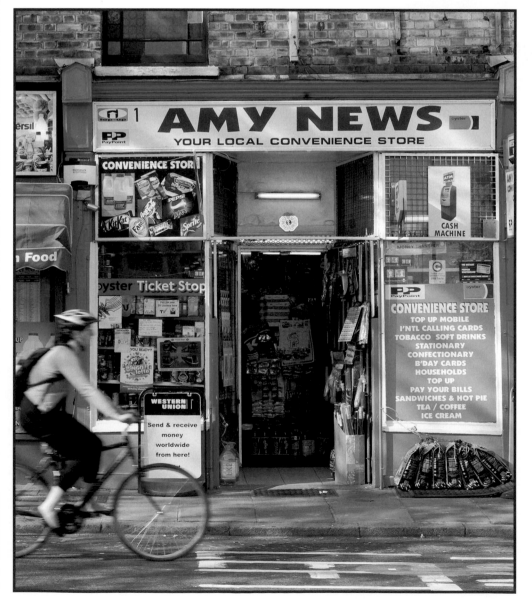

Some shops call themselves 'local convenience stores' because they stock all sorts of useful things for people who live in the nearby streets.

Can you name five things that this store sells and five services that it provides?

A local look

★ Draw a map showing the street where you live and the street where your nearest shop is.

★ Mark your house ✖ and the shop ✱ on the map.

★ Draw the quickest route from your house to the shop.

★ How many roads do you have to cross to get there?

Route to my nearest shop

★ Look at the chart below. What do you notice about the type of goods that the shops sells?

Convenience store goods

Food	Drinks	Newspapers and magazines	Stationery	Other

★ Talk about the goods your local shop sells.

★ List the items you have seen there.

★ Make a chart of your own.

★ Draw or find pictures of these items. Stick them onto your chart under the correct heading.

Local shops

Small, local shops are usually in a row called a parade. Each shop sells something different. There is often a food shop, a chemist, a newsagent, a dry cleaner, a hairdresser and a takeaway. These are all shops and services that people use very regularly.

A local look

★ Which things on this list does your family buy the most often?
★ Which can you find locally?
★ Where do you go to buy the other things?

A shopping list

- sticking plasters
- postage stamps
- a kebab
- a pair of trainers
- potatoes
- a T-shirt
- a bicycle helmet
- a dog collar
- a bunch of flowers

In big towns and cities, you can often find local shops selling food from other countries.

? What countries does food in these shops come from?

Supermarkets

A supermarket is a huge shop that stocks all the food and household goods that people need. Supermarkets attract many shoppers because their prices are cheaper than other shops.

Sainsbury's

We are open
Mon - Fri 7am - Midnight
Sat 7am - 10pm
Sun 11am - 5pm

How many hours is this supermarket open each day?

They often have large, free car parks outside. Shoppers can wheel trolleys full of shopping straight to their cars for loading.

A local look

★ Do a class survey to find out how long the journey is to the nearest supermarket. Put your data on a pie chart.

★ Does anyone walk there? How long does it take them?

★ Do another class survey to find out how often families visit the local supermarket. Use your data to make a block graph like this one.

★ Do families who live nearest the supermarket visit it most often?

Distance from the nearest supermarket

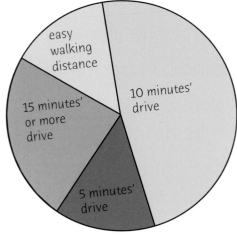

easy walking distance

10 minutes' drive

15 minutes' or more drive

5 minutes' drive

How often families visit the supermarket

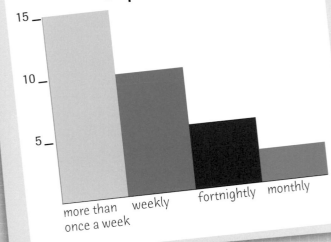

15 —
10 —
5 —

more than once a week   weekly   fortnightly   monthly

? What other facilities are there at the supermarket?

Cash machines

Fishmonger

Butcher

Delicatessen

The high street

High streets are usually wider than other streets in a town. They are lined with buildings on both sides. As well as shops, there may be hotels, offices, a post office and perhaps a museum or town hall.

? **Why are the buildings different shapes, heights and styles?**

SIGN OF THE PAST

Over time, shops often change their use. Signs and features may tell you what shops in your area sold in the past.

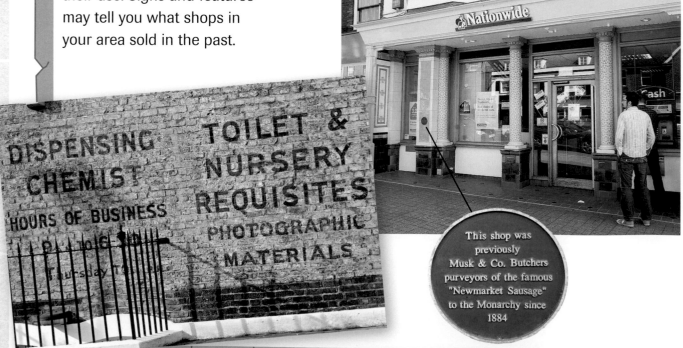

DISPENSING CHEMIST
HOURS OF BUSINESS
Thursday

TOILET & NURSERY REQUISITES
PHOTOGRAPHIC MATERIALS

Nationwide
Cash

This shop was previously Musk & Co. Butchers purveyors of the famous "Newmarket Sausage" to the Monarchy since 1884

A local look

This is a plan of all the buildings in a high street.

★ **Are there more clothes shops or places to eat and drink?**

★ **How many buildings are not shops or services?**

bank

baker

jeweller and watch mender

household goods

office

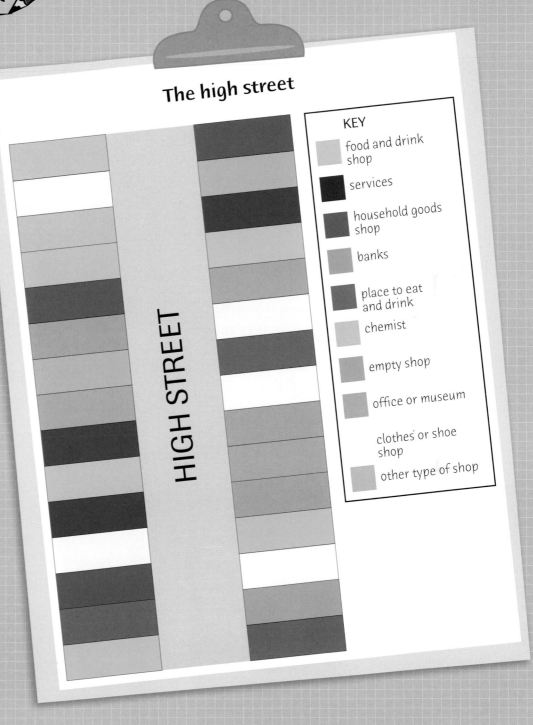

The high street

HIGH STREET

KEY

- food and drink shop
- services
- household goods shop
- banks
- place to eat and drink
- chemist
- empty shop
- office or museum
- clothes or shoe shop
- other type of shop

★ **Make a similar plan with photographs of your nearest high street. Colour code the use of different buildings.**

★ **How does your high street compare with this one?**

Markets

Outdoor markets take place once a week in small towns and more often in large towns.

MARKET PLACE
DERBYSHIRE DALES DISTRICT COUNCIL
PARKING IS PROHIBITED ON MONDAYS BETWEEN THE HOURS 5.00am AND 7.00pm
STALL MARKETS ARE HELD HERE EACH MONDAY

 When is market day in this town?

Stallholders lay out their stalls every morning and take everything away at night-time. They cram their stalls with as many goods as possible.

 Name three different things you could buy at this stall.

SIGN OF THE PAST

A market cross often marks the site of a market square.

Some markets have been held in the same spot for hundreds of years.

MARKET PLACE

 How do stallholders bring their goods to market and carry them away again?

Markets are often cheaper than shops.

What can you buy in a market for £1?

A local look

★ Make a list of the different stalls at a market and discover the most common goods that stalls sell.

★ Take photos of market displays. Notice how things are hung up and arranged. Compare how stalls differ from shop displays.

City centre shopping

Large towns and cities have a shopping area in the centre, with big shops and department stores. To attract shoppers, towns have closed some of the streets to traffic and made them into pedestrian shopping precincts.

 Spot these features of a pedestrian precinct in this photograph:
- seating
- litter bins
- trees
- advertising stands
- bollards.

If people drive to a city centre to shop, they need to find a place to park. Some towns provide buses to take people from a railway station or the outskirts to the centre. This helps reduce the amount of traffic in the city centre.

A local look

★ **Design a feature that would make your local shopping centre more attractive. Decide where you might put it.**

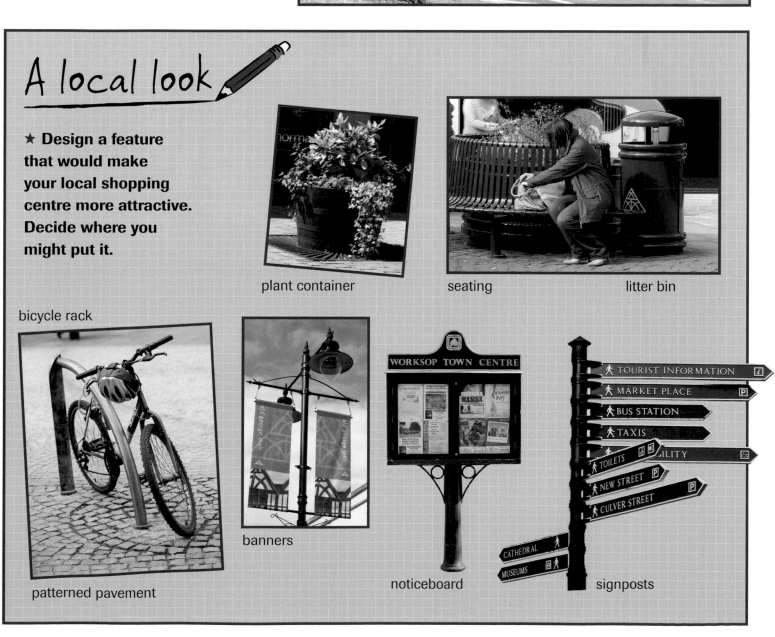

plant container

seating

litter bin

bicycle rack

patterned pavement

banners

noticeboard

signposts

Shopping malls

A shopping mall is a huge building with many different shops and stalls under one roof. It has a choice of places to eat and sometimes a cinema, as well. People visit malls to meet their friends, wander about or have a snack, as well as to shop.

perfume stall

 What are the umbrellas for? Why is it strange to have them inside?

A mall is warm and dry, which encourages shoppers to come in all weathers. The glass roof makes it feel light and airy.

The wide walkways have shops on both sides like a street. Benches, plants, and stalls help make the space look attractive.

Malls have their own car parks, so people do not have to walk far with their shopping.

A local look ✏️

★ **List the differences between a mall and a street of shops.**
★ **Which do you prefer? Why?**

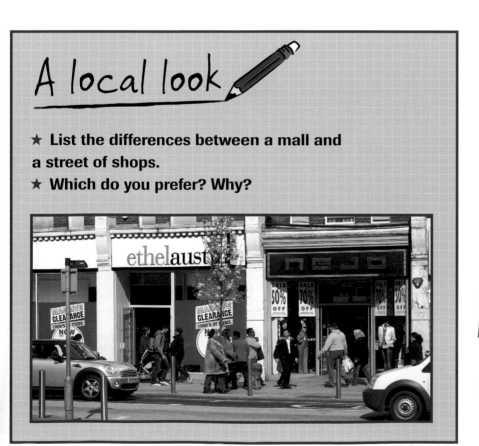

? **How does this mall shop entrance differ from one on a street?**

Retail parks

Large, modern shopping centres, called retail parks, have been built on the outskirts of towns and cities. The shops are so enormous, that they are known as superstores.

Superstores have space to display bulky goods, such as carpets, beds, sofas, sheds and cookers. People can choose them in the store and have the goods delivered to their homes.

Most people travel to retail parks by car. They can take home things small enough to fit in their car boot.

Retail parks are carefully planned to make shopping easy, safe and convenient.

★ Why does car parking take up most of the space?
★ Why are the superstores all arranged around the edges?
★ What else does this retail park have besides superstores?

★ Why is there a separate entrance for delivery trucks?
★ What makes the car park look attractive?

★ How did the planners make this retail park safe for pedestrians?

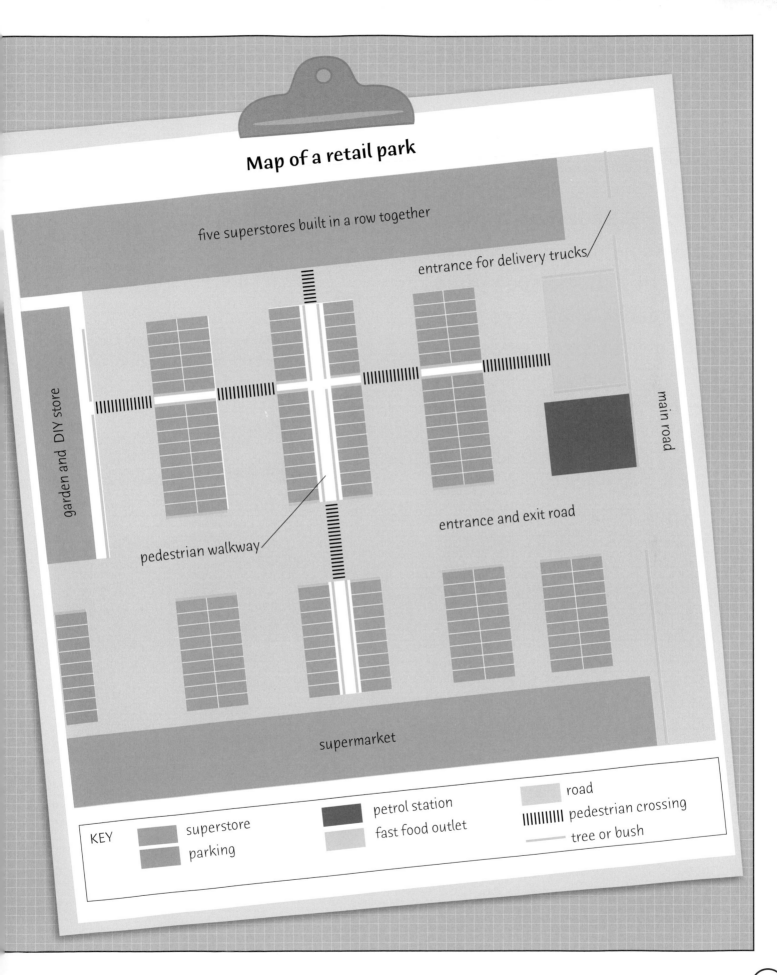

Map of a retail park

five superstores built in a row together

entrance for delivery trucks

garden and DIY store

main road

pedestrian walkway

entrance and exit road

supermarket

KEY
superstore
parking
petrol station
fast food outlet
road
pedestrian crossing
tree or bush

Specialist shops

Specialist shops sell one type of goods, such as musical instruments or jewellery. Shoppers may make a special journey to buy something particular in them. Specialist shopkeepers often know a lot about what they sell and can give shoppers advice.

? Why might you visit each of these shops? What could you buy there?

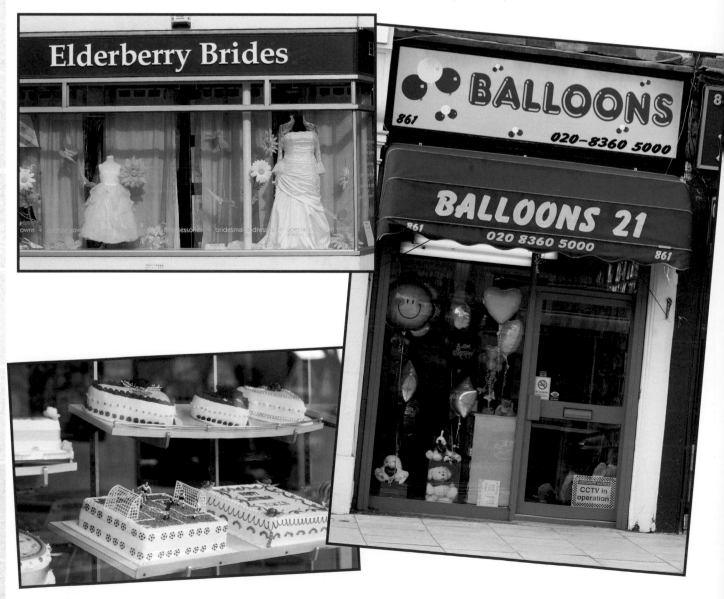

Some one-off shops reflect the place where they are. They stock souvenirs, local food and other goods especially for visitors. Other shops sell equipment for sports or hobbies.

? What clue does this sign give about the local area where this shop is?

? Where would you be likely to find people selling these things? What time of year do you think they are busiest?

A local look

★ Look for specialist shops in the place where you live. Find out what they sell.
★ Design a souvenir that would remind visitors of something in your local area.

Changes in shopping

Shopping is changing. Today, people can shop from home on the internet or on TV shopping channels. Some people swap goods instead of buying them. They can go to car boot sales to find cheaper, second-hand goods.

car boot sale

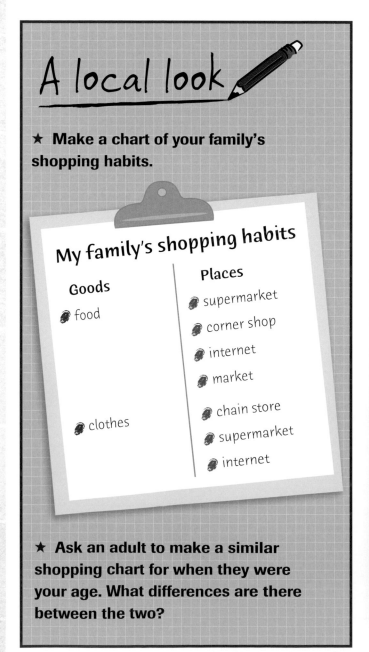

A local look

★ **Make a chart of your family's shopping habits.**

My family's shopping habits

Goods	Places
🖐 food	🖐 supermarket
	🖐 corner shop
	🖐 internet
	🖐 market
	🖐 chain store
🖐 clothes	🖐 supermarket
	🖐 internet

★ **Ask an adult to make a similar shopping chart for when they were your age. What differences are there between the two?**

Shopping is now a leisure activity. Friends and families often spend a whole day out together shopping.

pedestrianised shopping street

People use the internet to buy goods from all over the world or to order food from a supermarket. Van drivers deliver food from supermarkets to homes.

In the past, shops closed on Sundays and sometimes for a half-day in the week. Now big shops, supermarkets and superstores open every day and for longer hours than in the past. As shopping has changed, many small shops have closed down. Think about why this might be.

 How have the opening times of supermarkets and the range of goods and services they offer affected many high streets?

TESCO
Open
24 hrs
Mon 8am until Sat 10pm, Sun 10am - 4pm
Pharmacy
Recycling
Café

FOR SALE
ALL ENQUIRIES

More things to do

Take photographs or draw sketches of shops in your local area. Look at shop details.
★ What similarities or differences do you notice?
★ Which shops have the most colourful window displays?
★ Which have the largest outdoor displays?
★ Which are the busiest?

Find out about the food at local market stalls (especially at farmers' markets).
★ Has the trader produced it?
★ Is the produce local or has it come from faraway?
★ Can you plot on a map how far it has come?

People give things they no longer need to charity shops. These shops sell the goods to raise money for people in need.
★ Find out about charity shops in your area.
★ What is your nearest charity shop?
★ Find out about who or what the charity helps to support.

Investigate how easy it is for the elderly and people with wheelchairs or pushchairs to go shopping locally.
★ Are there any shop entrances that might be difficult for people like these?
★ Do any of the shops have automatic doors or ramps?
★ What has been done to help people with a disability?

Look for street names that tell you what was sold there in the past.

Find out which is the oldest shop in your area.
★ Does it sell the same sort of things now as in the past?

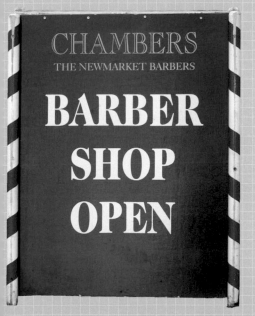

★ Look for old shop signs. Find out the origin of the barber's striped pole and the green cross for a pharmacy.

awning a cover that protects something from sun and rain

chain stores shops with the same name owned by the same company selling the same goods in different towns and cities

charity shop a shop that sells goods to raise money for a specific charity. Most of its goods are second-hand.

corner shop a small shop in an area of housing that sells many different sorts of everyday goods

customer someone who buys things from a shop or uses a service

department store a large shop, often on several floors, with separate departments, each selling different goods and services

fast food food that is quick to cook, such as kebabs, burgers and pizza

goods things that people buy and sell

greengrocer a shopkeeper who sells only fruit and vegetables

groceries food and household things, such as shampoo

parade a line of shops

pedestrian someone who makes a journey on foot

retail park a group of shops arranged around a huge car parking area

service something someone does for you, such as cut your hair

shopping mall a specially-built shopping centre, with lots of shops and cafés under one roof

shopping precinct an area of shops that is usually for pedestrians only

souvenir something people buy to remind them of a place or an event

stall a table or stand where things are laid out for sale

stock a store of goods in a shop or a warehouse

supermarket a large self-service shop that sells food and other goods

superstores huge supermarkets and shops

?Talking points

The questions in the book encourage close observation of the pictures and provide talking points for discussion.

Pages 4-5
• The shop signs are for a pharmacy, an optician and a fish and chip shop. Discuss other signs children might have noticed and explore how signs were used in the past, when few people could read.
• The services are key cutting; dry cleaning and laundry; shoe mending; printing photographs and haircutting. Can children think of others, such as clothes repairs, passport photos, nail bars and beauty salons?

Pages 6-7
• Shops attract customers by having: sales, where the price of goods is reduced; a display of goods outside the shop where customers can browse before going inside; a pavement sign which customers can see from a distance.
• Butchers never have outside displays for reasons of hygiene and to keep meat cool and fresh. Jewellery is too valuable to be left unattended outside.
• Discuss whether special offers might tempt people to buy more things than they really want or need.

Pages 8-9
• The store has a post office sign.
• The store sells newspapers, soft drinks, stationery, sweets, milk, tea, coffee, tinned food, wrapping paper, footballs, crisps, charcoal, sandwiches, hot pies and household goods.
• People can also send and receive money; get cash from a cash machine; top up mobile phones; buy a TV licence, a travel card, a lottery ticket and an international phone card and pay their bills. Discuss where else people could do these things.

Pages 10-11
• Encourage children to research the kinds of foods from other countries that are sold in this country. What vegetables and fruits are there? What sort of cakes and biscuits? What are the specialities of different countries?

Pages 12-13
This supermarket has a recycling centre on site as well as a cash machine and butcher, fishmonger and delicatessen counters inside the store. Customers can ask a shop assistant at these counters for exactly what they want. Think why this might be appealing compared with helping yourself for things from a shelf. In the past, all food shops had counters where they served customers.

Pages 14-15
• The buildings are different shapes, heights and styles because they were not all built at the same time.
• There are more clothes shops than places to eat or drink. Compare this ratio with shops in your area.
• There are four buildings that are not shops or services. Discuss what banks are and why they are in a high street.

Pages 16-17
• Market day in this town is on Monday. Find out about the history of the nearest market town. See what evidence of its past remains.

Pages 18-19
• Compare these pictures with the high street on page 14 and the shopping mall on page 20.

Pages 20-21
• Only cafés have umbrellas, an easily visible sign for customers. It is strange to have them open inside when people have no need to shelter here from sun or rain.
• The shop has no doors. Shutters come down at night.

Pages 22-23
• Parking spaces take up most of a retail park, because most people come by car. Find out whether buses also visit your nearest retail park and how they run.
• The stores are arranged around the edge, so customers do not have far to walk there from their cars. There is also a fast food outlet and a petrol station.
• Trucks go to the back of the store to load and unload.
• Trees and shrubs make the car park look more attractive.
• The walkways and zebra crossings across the entrance and exit road make the car park safer for pedestrians.

Pages 24-25
• People visit specialist shops now and again for special occasions, such as birthdays, weddings or to buy something for their work or hobby. Ask children what specialist shops they have visited or would like to visit.
• An angling shop is often found in places near rivers, where people who fish might need fresh supplies of bait.
• Traders sell shellfish and beach goods from stalls at the seaside, especially in summer when there are lots of holidaymakers.

Pages 26-27
• Individual shops never open for as long as supermarkets where people take turns to work in shifts. Customers who want to shop whenever they like may prefer to shop at supermarkets rather than at small shops. As shopping habits have changed, many high streets shops have closed down.